PUMPKIN PATCH

MADE WITH LOVE FOR

is for

APPLE

B is for

BONFIRE

MADE WITH LOVE BY

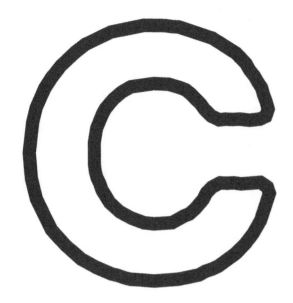

is for

CIDER

MADE WITH LOVE BY

D

is for

DONUT

MADE WITH LOVE BY

_____

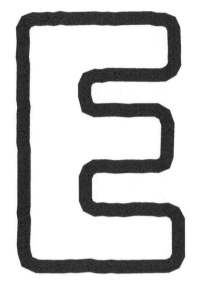

is for

EVERGREEN

F

is for

FLANNEL

F is for
FLANNEL

MADE WITH LOVE BY

is for

GOURDS

MADE WITH LOVE BY

is for

HAYRIDES

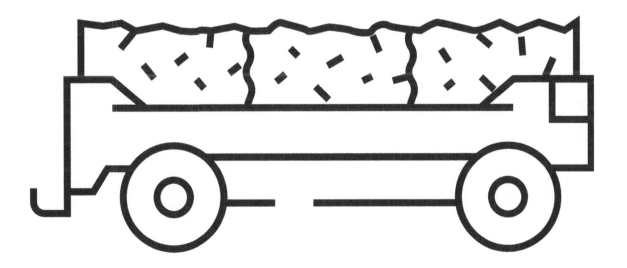

I

is for

INSECT

J

is for

JACK-O-LANTERN

MADE WITH LOVE BY

is for

KETTLE CORN

is for

LEAVES

MADE WITH LOVE BY

 is for

MAPLE SYRUP

MADE WITH LOVE BY

is for

NUTS

MADE WITH LOVE BY

is for

OWL

 is for

PUMPKIN

MADE WITH LOVE BY

P

PUMPKIN

MADE WITH LOVE BY

is for

QUILT

MADE WITH LOVE BY

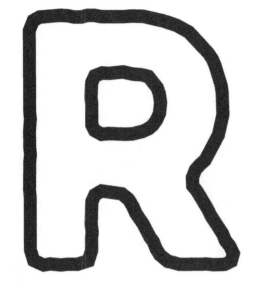

MADE WITH LOVE BY

is for

RAKE

S

is for

SCARECROW

MADE WITH LOVE BY

T

is for

TURKEY

MADE WITH LOVE BY

is for

UMBRELLA

MADE WITH LOVE BY

is for

VEST

MADE WITH LOVE BY

MADE WITH LOVE BY

is for

WAGON

 **is for**

X-RAY

MADE WITH LOVE BY

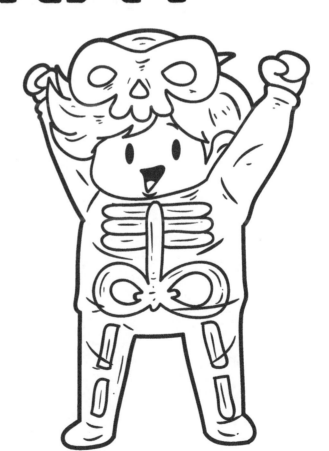

Y is for

YAM

MADE WITH LOVE BY

Z

is for

ZUCCHINI

Made in the USA
Las Vegas, NV
17 November 2024

11974201R00031